Hi, MoM!
Hi, DaD!

Hi, Mom! Hi, Dad!

101 Cartoons for New Parents
by Lynn Johnston

 **Meadowbrook Press**

Distributed by Simon & Schuster

New York

Library of Congress Catalog Number: 77-82216

Publisher's ISBN: 0-88166-189-9
Simon & Schuster Ordering Number: 0-671-78050-6

Published by Meadowbrook Press, 18318 Minnetonka Boulevard,
Deephaven, MN 55391.

BOOK TRADE DISTRIBUTION by Simon & Schuster, a division of
Simon and Schuster, Inc., 1230 Avenue of the Americas, New York, NY 10020.

97 96 95 94 93 92   6 5 4 3 2 1

Printed in the United States of America

The First Year of Life

A tiny bundle of life is placed in your arms, and at first it's hard to believe that you are now a parent. The overwhelming feeling of responsibility for another life, the pride and joy in your "creation," but also the concomitant feelings of inadequacy in your new role, frequently surface during that first year.

Lynn Johnston, with humor and sensitivity, creates cartoons that depict the feelings and reactions of parents as they learn to respond to the needs of the growing child, to the reactions of in-laws and relatives, to the pressures of the mass media, the experts, and the child-rearing fads. As we chuckle at the captions, we are reminded of the incredible amount of hardship experienced by parents during the baby's first year—the loss of sleep, the feeling of helplessness when the baby acquires new competencies and skills, as he or she learns to reach and grasp objects, sit up, creep, and finally becomes upright and mobile.

The baby becomes a "real" personality and enriches the life of the family. The joy experienced by the parents makes the struggle well worthwhile. The recognition of this joy is captured in the last cartoon: "To think that before we had a baby, this was just the same old park!"

With a few deft strokes of her pen, Lynn Johnston shows us what the first year of life is like. Her delightfully subtle cartoons at once make the hardships of life with baby more bearable.

MARY BLUM, PSYCHOLOGIST

8

11

12

13

14

15

16

19

21

22

23

24

26

30

32

33

34

36

I've tried feeding and rocking...and singing...and burping and bathing and pleading...and walking and shouting and whispering and... changing... and....

Dear Mom, you ask if we enjoy parenthood. Well, after 3 weeks of getting used to the situation, I can safely say ~~that we are already~~ that ~~things are that the baby is~~ Mom, can you make it out here?

LYNN

40

43

44

45

46

48

49

51

52

53

54

55

60

61

62

63

64

70

72

73

74

82

83

85

91

94

95

98

99

It's nice to be needed.

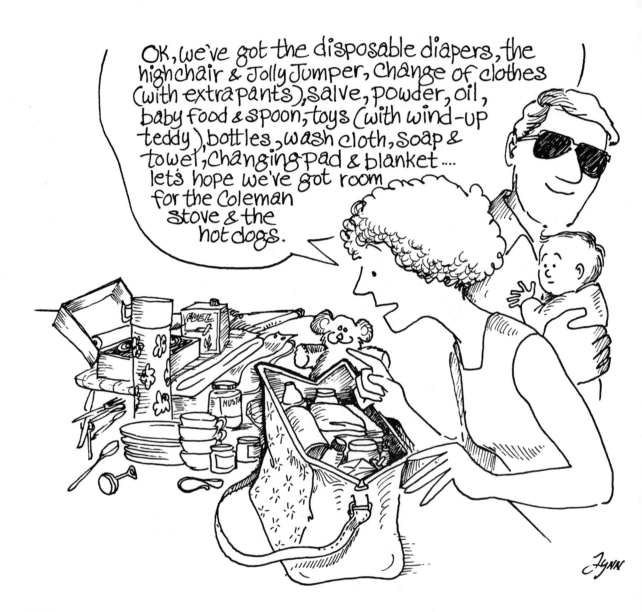

Meet Lynn Johnston

Lynn Johnston is North America's best-selling female cartoonist. She draws much of her material from close observation of her family: Aaron, Katie and husband Rod (a dentist). Lynn's deft, humorous depictions of life with kids have provided her with material for three books published by Meadowbrook Press, plus an internationally syndicated comic strip, *For Better or For Worse.* Lynn and her family live in Corbeil, Ontario.

& Her Books:

DAVID, WE'RE PREGNANT!

101 laughing-out-loud cartoons that accentuate the humorous side of conceiving, expecting, and giving birth. A great baby shower gift, it's the perfect way to bolster the spirits of any expectant couple.

Order # 1049

HI, MOM! HI, DAD!

A side-splitting sequel to *DAVID, WE'RE PREGNANT!* 101 cartoons on the first year of childrearing—all those late night wakings, early morning wakings, and other traumatic "emergencies" too numerous to list.

Order # 1139

DO THEY EVER GROW UP?

This third in her series of cartoon books is a hilarious survival guide for parents of the tantrum and pacifier set, as well as a side-splitting memory book for parents who have lived through it.

Order # 1089

OUR BABY'S FIRST YEAR

A Baby Record Calendar

A nursery calendar with
13 undated months for
recording "big events" of
baby's first year. Each
month features animal
characters, and baby care
and development tips.
Photo album page and family tree, too! A great
shower gift!

Order # 3179

THE PARENTS' GUIDE TO BABY & CHILD MEDICAL CARE

by Terril H. Hart, M.D.

A first aid and home
treatment guide that shows
parents how to handle over
150 common childhood ill-
nesses in a step-by-step
illustrated format. Includes a
symptoms index, health
record forms, child-proofing tips, and more.

Order # 1159

GRANDMA KNOWS BEST, BUT NO ONE EVER LISTENS!

by Mary McBride

Mary McBride instructs
grandmas who have been
stuck with babysitting how
to "scheme, lie, cheat, and
threaten so you'll be
thought of as a sweet, darling grandma."

Order # 4009

MOTHER MURPHY'S LAW

by Bruce Lansky

The wit of Bombeck and the
wisdom of Murphy are com-
bined in this collection of 325
laws that detail the perils and
pitfalls of parenthood.
Cartoon illustrations by
Christine Tripp.

Order # 1149

Order Form